The Treasure

Story re-told and illustrated by:

Michele Gentile

All the Best,

Michele ♡

Acknowledgements

I am deeply grateful to John Romano for so generously giving of his time, talent and encouragement to take my paintings and words and physically make a book out of them.

I am thankful for all the people who have touched my life, either for a reason, a season or a lifetime. Thank you for sharing your treasures with me.

Dedication

This book is dedicated to all the creative souls that come to this planet, and their infinite potential to make it a better place. This book is dedicated to *you*, your treasure within, all the good you have done so far, and all the good you will continue to do. May you experience the peace and joy of becoming ever greater versions of yourself.

This book is presented to:

_____

In honor of:

_____

Given by:

_____

This day of:

_____

The Treasure

Bear said,

"Give it to me, I will hide it in my cave."

The Creator said,

"No Bear, they will find it there."

Walrus said,

"Give it to me, I will hide it in the frozen land."

The Creator said,

"No Walrus, they will find it there too."

Llama said

"Give it to me, I will hide it on the top of the world."

The Creator said,

"No Llama, they will climb the mountains, and will even build cities there."

Dolphin said

"Give it to me, I will bury it on the bottom of the ocean."

The Creator said,

"No Dolphin, soon they will be able to go there too."

Eagle said

"Well then, give it to me, I will fly it to the moon!"

The Creator replied,

"Eagle, one day they will even go there."

Grandmother Mole who has no physical eyes but sees
with spiritual eyes said, *" Put it inside them."*
and the Creator said,

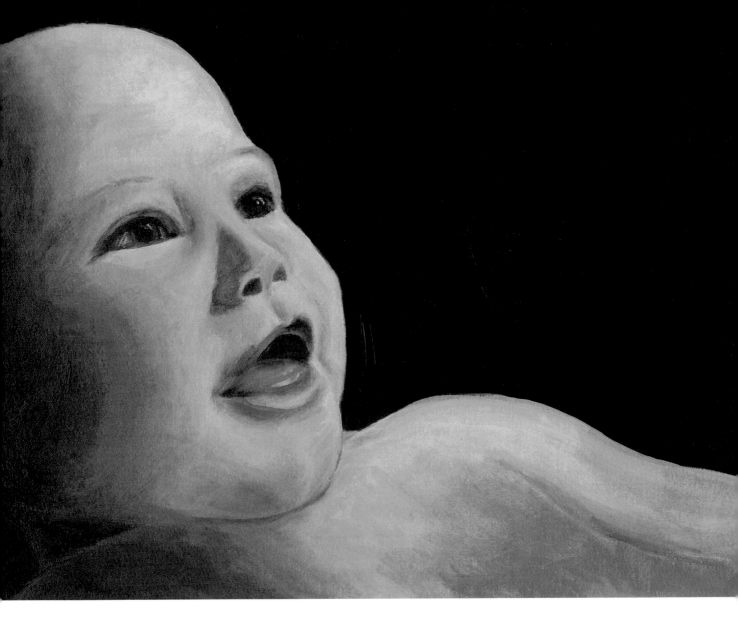

"It is done."

Why I made this book:

In 2001, I saw a version of this Sioux Indian myth in a corner of an OT newsletter. I was fascinated with the possibility of it *we create our own reality*. How? To what extent? I felt compelled to explore this idea further and to share this inspiring possibility with others.

I thought the best way to share this story, was as a beautifully illustrated book. There was one little problem with this idea, however. I was not an artist. I was a busy working mom with a full time life. The inspiration was so powerful though, that I took the project on anyway. Naively I began, learning through trial and error, taking a local drawing or painting class when I could, and reading many art books (I would have up to 40 books at my bedside at a time). And so it went for four years. Finally, 16 images were completed for my book, originally entitled "The Secret."

The paintings lay dormant until a dear friend, John Romano, came along and offered to make them into a book. He photographed, scanned, added the words to the images, punched tiny holes in the pages with an awl, hand sewed the pages together, made beautiful hardcovers and bound the books together. In October 2005, he presented me with ten handmade books. There was a display of my book in the public library and the local newspaper covered the story. It was one of the happiest moments of my life.

Since then, I have continued to explore the practical applications of "creating your own reality." I created a wellness textbook, written by experts, that tells how to improve our lives by taking care of our bodies, our minds, our finances, and our energy. I trained to become a life and wellness coach. As a result, my book evolved, too. This evolution resulted in a new version, called: The Treasure.

The Secret and The Treasure:

The story goes that we create our own reality. So what is the treasure? The treasure is *you*. I invite you to take a deep breath and pause to take that idea in. The treasure is you.

You may feel like you are a buried treasure, or an undiscovered treasure, or you may not feel like a treasure at all. But consider this: what's the difference between an acorn and a mighty oak tree, or a caterpillar and a butterfly?

The treasure that is you includes the qualities or "gifts" that you have to share with others. Your gift could be your interests, and how you develop them. Your gift can be your strengths. Your gift can be the qualities that have helped you to succeed in big ways or small. Your gift can be the love you share with others. Maybe you haven't found your gift yet, or maybe you haven't fully unwrapped it, but it is there for you to discover.

Is there something tugging inside you, something that wants to be expressed? Does it feel as if something is missing in your life? It could be a gift. In bringing it out you will have the joy of experiencing another facet of yourself. Some say that we are spirits who are having a human experience. The Treasure is about mastering the human experience and enhancing it with our spirit. As we explore and polish facets of our spirit, we become ever greater versions of ourselves. And deep down, I believe, that is what most of us really want. A glorious, powerful, and positive experience of ourselves. That is the treasure. The treasure is you.

To explore more about your treasures, and for free downloads, I invite you to visit: www.thetreasure.mobi

About Michele Gentile, MA, OTR/L, Wellness Coach

Michele has been a licensed occupational therapist for over 18 years. Occupational Therapy helps people to do the things they need to do regardless of any physical or mental obstacles they may encounter throughout their lifespan. It is a can-do approach based on the philosophy that people can influence their health and quality of their life through the process of engaging in activities that are meaningful to them.

Michele continued her study of health promoting behavior through two wellness coaching programs. Coaching is a process through which Michele helps her clients discover and experience more of what they want out of their life. She has coached people to: decrease their stress, improve their relationships, take charge of their health and wellbeing, begin a new career, lose weight and improve their fitness.

For more information please visit:
www.thetreasure.mobi